AF337283

Understanding Camus

"Understanding/graphic essay"
a collection directed by Luis de Miranda
© Max Milo éditions, Paris, 2024
www.maxmilo.com
ISBN 978-2-31501-271-8

Jean-François Mattei
Aseyn

Understanding Camus

Max Milo
COMPRENDRE/ESSAI GRAPHIQUE

Introduction
Misunderstanding of Thought

Camus was a **man of misunderstandings**. A misunderstanding with literary critics, who saw him as an adept of the absurd, when this was merely a stage in his development of thought. Misunderstandings with the academic world, which judged his philosophy with disdain, even though he made no claim to the title of philosopher. Misunderstanding with the Parisian world, which disliked him as an Algerian despite his intense love for the country of his birth. Misunderstanding with the French in Algeria, who saw him as an independentist, whereas he believed that Algeria could not do without France. Misunderstanding with the Arabs, who dismissed him as a colonialist when he denounced the injustices done to the natives. Misunderstanding with left-wing intellectuals who called him a reactionary when he was faithful to his libertarian commitments. And finally, he was misunderstood by those who

TOUTE TRAGÉDIE EST UNE TRAGÉDIE DE LA
RECONNAISSANCE

criticized him for preferring his mother to justice, even though he condemned the injustice of terrorists who could kill his mother.

But the initial, insurmountable misunderstanding was with this mother figure. Poor and widowed, she was deaf and almost mute. This illiterate housekeeper was incapable of reading her son's books. **It is this tragic situation that Camus transposes in his play *The Misunderstanding*.** An innkeeper's mother, who murders travelers in order to rob them, kills her son, whom she did not recognize on his return twenty years later. **Every tragedy is a tragedy of recognition.** And Camus was the one who was not recognized by his own people, even when he won the Nobel Prize. He was so distressed by this that he considered refusing the prize. And his entire body of work, which he considered barely begun, is marked by an **incompleteness frozen in fate** by his accidental death. No doubt he was aware of this when he wrote of *Premier Homme*, which he had been thinking about for years: "The book *must* be unfinished."

HE WANTED TO BUILD A WORK THAT WOULD PASS THROUGH THREE CYCLES: THAT OF THE ABSURD, THAT OF REVOLT, AND THAT OF LOVE. Faced with the strangeness of the world in which man appears, the first feeling experienced is that of the absurd. *The Stranger, The Plague* and *The Myth of*

« LE LIVRE DOIT ÊTRE INACHEVÉ. » ——

Sisyphus all highlight the absurdity of the human condition. It seeks to find meaning in a world devoid of it.

When man asks the question of being, **God's silence echoes the world's silence.**

The movement of revolt is born in the face of **human injustice**, which reinforces the misguidedness of history. *The Rebel*, les *Actuelles*, les *Chroniques algériennes* and Camus's political texts against all forms of totalitarianism legitimize the spontaneity of revolt. It is not confused, as Marxists would criticize, with revolution, which always ends in terror.

Man's journey was to end in the cycle of love. As with his misunderstanding, Camus transposed **his desperate love for his mother to the love of the world**. She could never return his love, locked away in her night, any more than he could feel the love of his father, who had died in the war. All he knew of him was a forgotten grave in the cemetery of Saint-Brieuc. *The First Man* is thus dedicated to the search for the father and to loyalty to the mother.

TO DISPEL THE MISUNDERSTANDINGS SURROUNDING THE HUMAN CONDITION, CAMUS SOUGHT A NEW PATH. He escaped the dialectics of Hegel and Marx, as well as the existentialism of Sartre and Merleau-Ponty, to return to a way of thinking born on the shores of the Mediterranean. Following in the footsteps of Nietzsche and Valéry, Camus speaks of

« LA VÉRITÉ DU MONDE »

"midday thought". It is not dedicated to knowledge, which is an imperative of reason, but to *recognition*, which is a requirement of the heart. La Pensée de midi is solar, and seeks its balance between the opposite poles of life. Camus' itinerary is thus one of refusal and consent, of yes and no, of measure and excess. Only this **constant balancing act** enables man to escape the nihilism of a Godless existence and become part of the "truth of the world".

I - Disquieting Strangeness

Freud detected in the "disquieting strangeness" of the familiar world, *das Unheimliche*, the unease that affects man's first certainties. Although Camus does not refer to the Viennese psychoanalyst, he constantly refers to this strangeness that each of us feels in the world to which we belong. A sentence from *The Myth of Sisyphus* is decisive in this respect: **"In a universe suddenly deprived of illusions and lights, man feels like a stranger."** This strangeness is closer to Pascalian dereliction than to Marxist alienation. As soon as man sets out in search of himself, as Socrates demanded with the imperative of the temple of Delphi, he discovers only his own labyrinths.

Deleuze used the term "conceptual character" to designate the fictional character who embodies a philosopher's ideas to the point of identification. In Camus's case, it's the **"mythical character"** who is his heteronym, and who the reader discovers in Ulysses, Prometheus or Sisyphus, before finding again in Meursault in *The Stranger* and Clamence in *The Fall*. Above all, **Ulysses is Camus' life model**. His last published work, *Exile and the Kingdom*, explicitly recalls the fate of Ulysses, who, after twenty years of exile, returns to his kingdom. But if the king of Ithaca could return to his island and regain his sovereignty, Camus feels an irremediable exile, since, as he remarks, **"he is deprived of the memories of a lost homeland or the hope of a promised land"**.

In a very Pascalian way, Camus experiences the eternal silence of these infinite spaces in the living desert of Florence or the dead city of Djémila (*Noces*). **This native strangeness of the world is** found in man himself, as soon as he observes that his thought can deny what it affirms, or affirm what it denies, without ever finding assurance. In *The Myth of Sisyphus*, the central sentence of the text echoes Ulysses' declaration to the Cyclops that his name is Outis, i.e. "Nobody". And Camus echoes this in his *Carnets* (vII, July 1954): **"Since always, someone in me, with all his strength, has tried to be nobody."**

As soon as thought comes into contact with the world and seeks a thread to guide it through its labyrinths, it comes up against its own walls without ever finding a way out. **Here, Camus returns to another myth, that of Plato's cave, in** which man is born amid shadows and simulacra. This is what *The First Man* calls the **"obscure**

«DANS UN UNIVERS SOUDAIN PRIVÉ D'ILLUSIONS
ET DE LUMIÈRES, L'HOMME SE SENT
UN ÉTRANGER.»

part of being", as if each of us, not content with living among shadows, were himself lined with shadows. Plato believed that there was a way out of the cave, and that the prisoner could free himself and enter the higher world of Ideas and Forms. **Like Nietzsche, Camus does not believe in backward worlds.** True to his Mediterranean inspiration, he worships the rawness of light, but knows he is condemned to the threat of shadow.

In a belated preface to his matrix work, *The Wrong Side and the Right Side*, the author holds the scales equally between the two poles of his existence. **"I was placed halfway between misery and the sun. Misery prevented me from believing that all is well under the sun and in history; the sun taught me that history is not everything."** Here we recognize the constant balancing of Camusian thought, the rhythm of which is set by his poetic prose. **The world teaches us that light is balanced by shadow,** life by death, upside down by right side up, so that clear-cut oppositions balance each other out, leaving man in a state of expectation. As with Heraclitus, for whom the way up and the way down are one and the same, opposites form the intimate fabric of a world that knows no higher resolution.

All Camus's stories, featuring these mythical characters who are the author's doubles, follow

the same pattern. That of a search for meaning that only leads to a final impasse. The narrator of *The Stranger*, Meursault, learns from a telegram from the asylum that his mother has died: **"Today, Mom died. Or maybe yesterday, I don't know."** He remains a total stranger to the news, and feels no emotion whatsoever. The mythical character reveals Camus's own personality. He loved his mother with a desperate love that she was unable to return, deaf and stubborn, forever locked in her silence. And this lack of recognition gave him a **sense of strangeness that never left him**. Meursault, the man without a first name, and therefore, for a Christian, the man without an identity, seems to feel nothing for his mother, his mistress or his friends. Camus's white writing, imitating American novelists, sketches the portrait of a character devoid of interiority.

The climax of the story is the **crime scene on the beach in Algiers**. The narrator has no reason to follow his friend Raymond, who is looking for an Arab to avenge an offense. Meursault thinks only of avoiding the scorching sun that falls vertically on the sand. But when the brutal light coming from the sky, the same light as the one at his mother's funeral, blinds Meursault, this character woven of *Sea* and *Sun*, he shoots this unknown Arab five times for no apparent reason. **He will only note, in a tone of vague**

regret, that he has destroyed the balance of the day. The same indifference to his fate is to be found when Meursault is in prison. He has been condemned to death, but feels no sense of fear or revolt. He is locked in a cell, talking to himself as he discovers his face in the reflection of an iron bowl. He only reveals his emotions at the end of the novel, when he refuses the help of the chaplain who has taken pity on his "blind heart". He doesn't want anyone's help, because he himself is "no one": he is **content to confide before he dies**—and Camus's formula is decisive here—**in the "tender indifference of the world"**.

The same strangeness surrounds the narrator of *The Fall*. This conceptual character also bears a significant name: **Jean-Baptiste Clamence**, referring to the prophet who announced the coming of Jesus by preaching in the desert, ***vox clamans in deserto*** (John, I, 23). Unlike Meursault, Clamence has an inner life that he delights in dissecting in an interminable monologue. This Parisian lawyer who has taken refuge in Amsterdam proudly **proclaims** his faith in himself, as if to stifle the cry that has obsessed him for years. One night, while crossing a bridge in Paris, **he heard the scream of a woman who had fallen into the Seine,** but didn't stop. Since then, he has heard a kind of laughter that pursues him, like an echo

« AUJOURD'HUI, MAMAN EST MORTE.
OU PEUT-ÊTRE HIER, JE NE SAIS PAS. »

of the original cry. No one answered John the Baptist in the desert of Judea; this time, in the desert of Amsterdam, **it was John the Baptist who failed to answer the call of a drowning woman.**

THE FALL IS EVEN MORE SIGNIFICANT OF THE STRANGENESS OF EXISTENCE than *The Stranger*. The first titles planned for this story were **The Last Judgment**, then **The Scream**. We are reminded of Munch's painting, which the Norwegian painter wrote in his *Diary* in memory of **"an infinite cry that passed through the universe and tore nature apart"**, as he went for a walk one evening. It was also the cry of Jesus on the Cross, and his unanswered call to abandonment by his Father. Camus' character, and doubtless Camus himself, is haunted by this call in the silence of the night, and by the judgment that sanctions the life of every man. The tragedy of existence, which no one has willed and from which no one can escape, even if it means suicide, consists in the silence that follows every call. And for Camus, as for Clamence, **the call is always a call for meaning in a world devoid of it**.

Amsterdam, where Clamence has taken refuge in the belief of escaping the cry, just as Cain locked himself in the tomb to escape the eye of God, is a representation of Hell. The narrator makes a precise reference to *The*

Il constatera simplement, sur un
ton de vague regret, qu'il a
détruit l'équilibre du jour.

Divine Comedy: **"The concentric canals of Amsterdam resemble the circles of Hell. Here, we are in the last circle."** Indeed, Clamence lives in his own hell, which is nothing other than self-enclosure with no possibility of escape. Every day, he suffers the weight of his past guilt, which is all the more haunting because he can't go back. Lady Macbeth's bloodstain was indelible; the abandoned woman's cry will be just as unforgettable.

But *The Fall* is not Clamence's only trial. It is also the trial of the "penitent judges", as the narrator defines himself. **These beautiful souls who, in judging themselves, beat their culpas on the chest of others**, are the progressive intellectuals of Camus's time. The story thus has both political and moral stakes. Its author rejects the illusions of the *Modern Times* left, Jean-Paul Sartre and the existentialists, and the moral posture that these penitent judges seek to impose on the world by remaining deaf to the appeal of the victims of communism in the era of the Soviet empire. **Clamence, who is the image of Sartre**, but also, in certain respects, that of Camus, puts himself on trial to better accuse other men of his impotence. The intellectuals of our time, who have taken the place once occupied by theologians and philosophers, are for Camus nothing but false prophets. Unlike

« UN PARTISAN ÉCLAIRÉ DE LA SERVITUDE »

Saint John the Baptist, **they only proclaim the coming of salvation for mankind in their own desert**.

This desert, common to all men, is that of servitude. For Camus, the strangeness of the human condition manifests itself in a willing submission to servitude. Etienne de La Boétie wrote the *Contr'Un*, which was defined as a "discourse on voluntary servitude". Camus discerns, beneath the mask of justice of the intellectuals who submit to the Communist dictatorship by refusing to admit the existence of the Soviet camps, a **strange adherence to servitude**. The hero of *The Fall*, speaking to an imaginary interlocutor, similarly recognizes himself as an **"enlightened supporter of servitude"**. The word "enlightened" is a terrible one here, since it evokes the "Enlightenment" of reason that progressivism has always claimed for itself. And Camus justifies his criticism by noting in his *Carnets* (VII, 1952) what he thinks of the intellectuals of *Modern Times*: **"Something in them, in the end, aspires to servitude."**

Where does this paradoxical taste for servitude come from, if not this choice of "happiness in slavery", to use Jean Paulhan's expression in his presentation of *Histoire d'O*? From the absence of a true master who would enable men to find their right path. For Camus, man's dereliction stems from the absence of God, which he himself experienced as the absence of his father, who died in the war. ***The First Man* provides the key to this enigma.** This novel, unfinished by the author's death, opens with the "Search for the Father", who will remain absent forever. In the same text, he says of his generation: **"As children without God or father, we were horrified by the masters we were offered."** Camus is thinking here of Hegel, Marx or Stalin, the "Little Father of the Peoples", before whom political conformism genuflected. Modern times, whose ethical and religious principles were destroyed by world wars and death camps, have only reinforced the strangeness of a world that calls for meaning, but lacks it.

We are all godless and fatherless, unable to conquer true mastery. Camus' tragic vision stems from this damning observation: when the masters have disappeared, comes the time of tyrants who give men only one assurance: that of servitude. We are reminded of Lacan's words to the students at Vincennes in 1968: **"What you as revolutionaries aspire to is a master. You'll have him!"**

II - Double Game of the Absurd

CAMUS DISCOVERED THE ABSURD WHEN HE DISCOVERED THE WORLD. The Latin word *ab-surdus* means "discordant" and evokes a **break in harmony and musical dissonance**. This out-of-tune sound comes from a world that appears to obey a rigorous order, but is in fact devoid of chords and unison. As the short story "L'énigme" in *L'Été* puts it, however, the absurd is only a **"starting position"** in Camus's itinerary. It will continue through the stages of revolt and love. If the world is absurd, because it does not meet man's expectations, it remains possible to harmonize it as a composer resolves an initial dissonance with a perfect chord.

As a result, and here Camus advances a controversial theme, **"there is only one really serious philosophical problem: suicide"**. He poses the question of being and non-being on the concrete plane of existence, not on that of theoretical abstraction. Only a being that *is* can suppress its being, showing by its act that being commands nothingness, and nothingness commands being. But then, just as **being and nothingness form an inseparable fabric, so life and death constitute the other side of existence**. It's impossible to separate them, to desire being while refusing non-being. Such is the absurdity of the world, but at the same time its intelligibility: every opposition that comes to being is accompanied by non-being. And it is this link, which binds death to life, that we deem absurd because we don't know how to balance opposites.

THE ABSURD DEVELOPS IN TWO STAGES. The first is man's fundamental concern with *unity*, whether of the world, the city or his own life. Camus was strongly influenced by Plotinus' theory of the One who governs all things, the multiplicity of beings being only an appearance. His post-graduate diploma in philosophy was devoted to a comparison of the thought of Saint Augustine and the metaphysics of Plotinus. And **this major theme of unity—ontological, moral and political—was to dominate Camusian thought**. But secondly, neither the world nor God can satisfy this concern for unity. As Baudelaire put it: "What is the fall? If it is unity that has become duality, it is God who has fallen" (*Mon cœur mis à nu*, aphorisme 162). This religious theme of the fall obsessed

LA VIE ET LA MORT CONSTITUENT
L'ENVERS ET L'ENDROIT DE L'EXISTENCE.

Camus, even though he was a non-believer. It's not a fall out of paradise, but a fall out of unity, in the manner of Plotinus. From then on, **"it is up to man to create a unity for himself, either by turning away from the world, or within the world"** (*Carnets*, IV, 1942).

The double game of the absurd can be recognized by the fact that, on the one hand, man expects a unity fragmented by the multiple, and that, on the other, this expectation is disappointed by the absence of unity, whether due to the will of God or the indifference of the world. We can then understand the decisive sentence of *The Myth of Sisyphus*: **"The absurd is this divorce between the spirit that desires and the world that disappoints, my longing for unity, this dispersed universe and the contradiction that chains them together."** The major work in this respect, from 1939 onwards, is *Noces*, whose title reveals the essence of Camus's thinking. He desires with all his might to unite with the world, just as he desires with all his might to unite with his mother, and, even more generally, to unite with men, as shown by the play on words he makes in his short story "Jonas ou l'Artiste au travail" (*Exile and the Kingdom*), between ***solitaire*** and ***solidaire***, separated by a single vowel. But instead of celebrating a wedding with the world and mankind, **we're invited to a divorce with mankind and the world.**

What, then, is the absurd? In Being and Time, Heidegger spoke of an "existential", which is not an accidental character, but an essential structure of the human condition. The Greeks, first and foremost Plato and Plotinus, bequeathed to us the idea of the *cosmos*, i.e. **a world ordered by reason in the least of its aspects**, so that all its elements, and first and foremost the human element, are consonant like the chords of a symphony. The Stoics thus spoke of a **system of Earth and Sky, Men and Gods**, governed by the universal *logos*. Modern thinkers, such as Leibniz, Hegel and Marx, have attempted to rediscover this systematicity of the world, based on a single principle—God in Leibniz, Spirit in Hegel or Matter in Marx—in a rational, dialectical network that unifies contradictions. But for Camus, who does not believe in a system, this unity that man hopes for remains an illusion. **Man and the world will always be fragmented, and the divorce between them will be forever consummated.**

Camus uses two metaphors to evoke the absurd. **That of the world's *visibility* and that of its *silence*,** giving equal weight to looking and listening. The absurd is first and foremost the **weight of silence** that the world echoes back to us as we speak to it. Camus emotionally experienced the anguish of such silence through his mother's silence. The more he addressed her, first and foremost in his writings since *The Wrong Side and the Right Side* where her presence is constant, the less response he heard. The dedication of *The First Man* to his illiterate mother bears witness to this: "**À toi qui ne pourras jamais lire ce livre**" (**"To you who will never be able to read this book"**). The mother's silence is the matrix of the silence of the universe. But the absurd is also to be found in the **thickness of visibility** that the world offers us. The sea, the sun, the skies and mountains, the grandeur and beauty of the landscape all seem to send us signs that we can't decipher, despite the painters and poets. Our eyes are filled with emotion at the beauty of beings, but we never manage to decipher what these appearances show and conceal.

MAN MUST THEN MAKE A CHOICE. To live in submission, without understanding it, to the incessant play of phenomena that appear only to disappear soon. Or to live by trying to balance what is temporal with what is eternal. Camus doesn't believe in God, or, as Nietzsche put it, in an "afterworld"; people are born, live and die in this world, with no hope of escape. We'll never get out of the cave. **But we can feel that part of the eternal that we carry within us, and which is manifested in artistic**

L'ABSURDE EST D'ABORD CETTE PESANTEUR
DE SILENCE.

creation. When the painter or sculptor completes his work, it is like a suspension of time in its trace of eternity. As Spinoza put it, "we feel and experience that we are eternal" (Ethics, V, XXIII). This test of eternity is that of art or thought, which tears itself away from the ceaseless passage of time in an attempt to overcome it.

Camus does not meet God in this false eternity. Agnostic rather than atheist, he remains on the razor's edge of existence, between being and nothingness, the other side of things and the other side of things, asking the world for an answer it won't give him. **And the question is indeed that of God**. Camus is fascinated, ontologically and ethically, by the terrible words of Ivan Karamazov in Dostoyevsky's novel *Demons*, which he adapted for the stage in 1959 under the title *The Possessed*. The main character exclaims that if God doesn't exist, **"everything is permissible"**. The conclusion of the implicit syllogism—God forbids evil deeds; there is no God; therefore all deeds, including evil ones, are permissible—is irrefutable. But then, on what basis do we judge a given act to be evil, or criminal, and what right do we have to forbid it and punish its perpetrator? If there is no longer a universal commandment ordering what is permitted and forbidden, right and wrong, how can we justify existence in a transient world where everything is constantly changing and modifying? **Where are the**

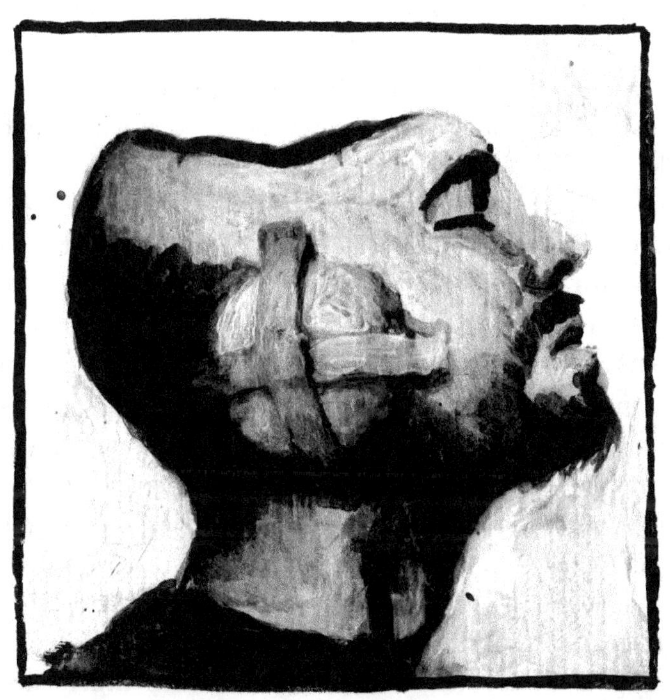

« LES HOMMES MEURENT ET NE SONT PAS HEUREUX. »

Tables of the Law that tell us what's right, and who's in charge of writing them?

For Ivan Karamazov, as for Camus, the realization that "anything goes" brings together the absurdity of the world and man's renunciation of it. If he sacrifices himself to this false liberation, he will sever the ties that bind him to the world and to mankind. And he will ultimately die in despair. This is what is implied by Caligula's bitter observation in the play of the same name: **"Men die, and they are not happy."** The Roman emperor's excess can be seen in his absurd desire to become a god and experience the happiness of the Immortals. But pagan gods are no happier than men, and are indifferent to their fate. As for the Christian god, he died on the cross to redeem mankind's sins, and was not happy, but abandoned by his Father. The absurdity of existence is born of this conflict between the desire to last that man discovers deep within himself, and the reality of his impending demise, the reason for which he does not understand. This is why Caligula argues that **"men weep because things are not as they should be"**.

And they are not what they should be, because some things are unbearable in their cruelty and gratuitousness, as if evil had the right to come to our table and take from us what is our most precious possession. THIS MOST PRECIOUS

GOOD IS LIFE. Camus shows us this in a famous episode from *The Plague*. Dr. Rieux has tried in vain to save a small child stricken by the epidemic that is devastating Oran. **But the child agonizes with a final cry of suffering, leaving both the doctor and the priest at his bedside speechless.** If we must love what we cannot understand, for the priest, we cannot admit the unjust death of a child for the doctor. **"This death, at least, was innocent,"** cries Dr. Rieux, outraged by a death he was unable to prevent. **The absurd is less the scandal of death and injustice than man's incomprehension of his powerlessness to perpetuate life.**

To express the cosmic, and therefore universal, dimension of the absurd, Camus needed another **mythical figure,** and not just a conceptual one like Dr. Rieux, Meursault or Jean-Baptiste Clamence. He called on **Sisyphus, not a god but a mortal**, the most cunning of them all, who had been condemned by Zeus to eternally climb a boulder to the top of a mountain in the Underworld. At the very top, the boulder tumbled down from the summit into the abyss, and Sisyphus had to climb back down again, without a moment's rest. **Sisyphus is not the mythical figure who embodies revolt; that function belongs to Prometheus.** On the contrary, he is the hero of consent to existence. However hard life may be, precisely because he lives and has no other choice, man must want to coincide with what life gives him, that is, with himself.

The weight of existence is undoubtedly too heavy to be renewed every day, like the gesture of Sisyphus. Yet wisdom dictates that we serenely accomplish our task, which has been assigned to us by the gods or the world, and which we cannot refuse without going overboard. Indeed, the most absurd thing would be to ask the world to stop being itself in order to become something else, as if life offered us this possibility. ***The Wrong Side and the Right Side* features this implacable sentence that expresses Camus's realism: "To change life, yes, but not the world of which I made my divinity."** Paradoxically, then, man must consent to the absurd if he is to rebel against a life that deprives him of his humanity. This is the second cycle of the Camusian itinerary, which begins with the absurd and leads to love through revolt.

« LE MONDE DONT JE FAISAIS MA DIVINITÉ. »

III - Justifying Revolt

Descartes based knowledge on the intuitive grasp of his thought: "I think, therefore I am", by putting the world in doubt. Camus, explicitly alluding to the author of the *Discourse of Method*, bases morality on the intuitive grasp of his revolt: **"I revolt, therefore we are"**, by putting history in doubt. For revolt is not a *worldly* process that attacks things themselves; it is a *historical* process that rises up against human injustice. Camusian revolt thus becomes as methodical as Cartesian doubt. But unlike Descartes, who was isolated in his self-reflection: **"therefore *I* am"**, Camus' itinerary leads him towards other men: **"therefore *we* are"**. Revolt is, from the outset, an opening onto the universal. We can be indignant alone, but we can only revolt in the company of other men.

Like the absurd, from which it springs, **revolt has a dual nature**. It says "no" to the acts of injustice that are intolerable to it, but it says "yes" to the gestures of love that bind it to men. Camus is all about what he calls the "**balancing act**" between affirmation and negation, or refusal and consent. Already, suicide, which illustrated the absurd, was both a refusal of life and a consent to death. **Revolt, which stems from the absurd, will be both refusal of injustice and consent to humanity**. This duality reflects that of man, always torn "between yes and no", "between upside down and right side up", or "between measure and excess", to use Camus's constant play on contrasts. Rebellion thus rejects human injustice and the world's silence, while consenting to the **beauty of things and the truth of the good**.

Camus can then make a radical distinction between revolt, which finds consent at the heart of its refusal, and revolution, which denies consent at the heart of its refusal. The former is affirmative, the latter nihilistic, and the whole of *The Rebel* is founded on this distinction. Camus will show that "**revolt is not originally the total negation of all being**", as the violence of all revolutions testifies; "on **the contrary, it says yes and no at the same time**". The man in revolt, with whom Camus identifies both in his work and in his life, while rejecting the darkness of history, also accepts, "**from his very first movement**", Camus points out, man's moral duality and his share of clarity, which must be recognized, protected and loved.

« JE ME RÉVOLTE, DONC NOUS SOMMES »

The world and history must be brought face to face. If the world has nothing to do with the history of mankind, for it was there before them and will survive them, **history must admit the primacy of the world and consent to its indifference**. We must therefore accept the death that existence imposes on us, since everything that comes to be, from the gigantic stars to our tiny planet, is doomed to nothingness. But if we *cannot* rise up against the world, we *must rise up* against history when it jeopardizes humanity's very existence and the principles of justice that are essential to it. **Where revolution, in its intoxication with negation, betrays the human ideal of freedom by providing a breeding ground for terror, revolt, by balancing the "no" with the "yes", consent to the good with the refusal of evil, succeeds in combining man's need for order with his demand for freedom.**

Revolt is not simply an ethical category that would make Camus a traditional moralist. He has been sufficiently criticized for the "moraline", as Nietzsche put it, that would impregnate his work to the point of making him a philosopher for the final year of high school. **It's an ontological category, like the absurd, which expresses the confrontation between man and the world in an affective mode.** In *The Myth of Sisyphus,* Camus writes that revolt brings man face to face with "his own obscurity" in his demands, and here we find a new contrast, of "impossible transparency". Camus has worked on St. Augustine, as he has on Rousseau and Nietzsche, and he knows nothing of man's efforts to illuminate his own abyss. But while the *Confessions* bear witness to man's desire to achieve self-transparency, they always fail to reveal a being. Saint Paul asserted that we can only see ourselves in a **"dark mirror"**, whereas in God we see ourselves **"face to face"**. Camus doesn't believe in God, and therefore thinks that transparency is impossible. What **remains is to use revolt as the outward revelation of a human dignity that is impossible to fathom.**

By rebelling, precisely because his protest movement is both refusal and consent, **man discovers within himself that *ethical limit*, that of the Good, which men must not transgress.** An anecdote from the life of Camus's father illustrates this point. He was in Morocco for his military service, and had seen a French sentry's throat slit during an uprising by independence fighters, with his genitals at the back of his throat. To one of his comrades, who, without rebelling, observed that it was the Moroccans' custom to mutilate their enemies, because they believed they were acting "like men", Camus' father exclaimed: **"No, a man can't do that. That's what a man is, or else...".** A high-school philosopher would have offered his readers an analysis of the Kantian categorical imperative to justify the universality of the moral law. Camus's father, a farm laborer, had protested on the basis of immemorial wisdom: there are things a man forbids himself to do. **There's no need to appeal to God or the Moral Law.** All you have to do is listen to your heart and feel what you ought to do, not consent to what you've done wrong.

REVOLT REVEALS MAN'S HUMANITY, IF ONLY IN A DARK MIRROR. Camus uses the **mythical figure of Prometheus to symbolize what he calls "metaphysical revolt".** For disobeying Zeus and loving the men to whom he brought fire, Prometheus is chained to a column on the edge of the Caucasus. An eagle eternally gnaws at his liver, which grows back as it grows. Camus rightly notes that the **rebellious Titan does not rise up against all creation, but against Zeus alone,** and that he has consented in return to his love of mankind. Zeus, moreover, forgives him and sets him free in the rest of the myth. And yet, Prometheus' eternal suffering is mirrored in human history. "For twenty centuries", writes Camus, **"the sum total of evil has not diminished in the world",** and **"no parousia, either divine or revolutionary, has been accomplished".**

What, then, is man, subjected to all forms of injustice? The second *Letter to a German Friend* offers this definition:

« VOILÀ CE QU'EST UN HOMME, OU SINON... »

"He is that force which always ends up balancing tyrants and gods." Here, implicitly using the image of Prometheus, Camus uses a mythical metaphor to attack another myth, this one recent and non-religious, that of Nazism. Zeus was content to impose torture on a single victim; Hitler will impose suffering on whole swathes of humanity. The Germans who sank into *hubris* believed that there was no "higher reason" than man, and that, in the absence of God, the superior race could destroy the inferior races. But if there is no transcendence, it does not follow that all actions are permissible and equivalent. **The Nazis didn't believe in "the meaning of this world"** and deduced that, in history, "good and evil" bend in all directions according to the force that drives them. This ontological nihilism will destroy itself, and history will rise up in revolt against those who have despaired of the world and humanity.

Camus' revolt against suffering and death justified his **radical rejection of the death penalty and the atomic bomb.** In 1957, along with Arthur Koestler and Jean Bloch-Michel, he contributed to the polemical *Réflexions sur la peine capitale*. Camus' text, with the more scathing title *Réflexions sur la guillotine*, was published separately and should have served as the conclusion to *The Rebel*. Camus then opted for a more optimistic ending with his analyses of the Pensée de midi, which opened up a path "beyond nihilism". He had already staged the guillotine at the end of *The Stranger* and *The Fall,* when **Meursault and Clamence defiantly exclaim that, with their execution, "all will be consummated!"** Camus now attacks him head-on in memory, once again, of his father. He had learned from his family that this unknown father was a supporter of the death penalty. Outraged by the murder of children, he had wanted to attend the public execution of the killer in Algiers. **When he returned home, he didn't say a word to his wife and suddenly started vomiting.** It was this primitive scene, as psychoanalysis would say, that forever marked the child's mind and enabled him to associate the image of the unknown father with death.

Revolt against evil cannot be confused with what Nietzsche called the "spirit of vengeance". And we cannot respond to death with death, as if resentment against the criminal should take precedence over resentment against humanity. The Second World War multiplied atrocities in Europe and around the world. The victory of Nazism and the forces of the Rome-Berlin-Tokyo axis threatened to destroy millions of men and impose on the survivors the "Thousand-Year Reich" announced by Hitler. **But on August 6, 1945, the United States**

dropped the first bomb on the city of Hiroshima to end the war. It effectively ended the lives of almost two hundred and fifty thousand civilians. Three days later, **a second bomb was dropped on the city of Nagasaki**, killing seventy-five thousand inhabitants and mortally wounding the same number of civilians.

On August 8, between the two bombs, Camus published **a protest against this crime against civilians.** The article began with the words: "Le monde est ce qu'il est, à savoir peu de chose". And the author went on to use irony, the most refined form of revolt, by casually pointing out that "any medium-sized city can be totally wiped out by a bomb the size of a soccer"! He went on to condemn not just the bomb, but the "indecency" of those celebrating the success of a military operation in the service of "the most formidable rage for destruction that man has displayed in centuries". **Rejecting the right of "mechanical civilization" to reach "its last degree of savagery"**, Camus was the only intellectual of his time to speak out against the use of atomic weapons against civilian populations. Faced with the "terrifying prospects" that threatened to put an end to humanity while destroying nature, Camus wagered on a peace that was the only battle worth fighting.

But to conquer this peace, which would allow man to choose "between hell and reason", the **only path to**

« L'ESPRIT DE VENGEANCE »

la seule voie à suivre ——————

follow is that of revolt. If man can never measure himself against the world, despite his science and technology, he can measure himself against history and try, not to change it, but to give it meaning. By refusing both the injustice of history and the silence of the world, man in revolt, like Prometheus, consents to **the beauty of the earth and the justice of mankind.**

IV - Betrayal of the Revolution

When revolt radicalizes into revolution, it turns against itself and betrays its own ideals of justice. Marx had said that it is men who make history, even if they don't know the history they are making. And this history, as Marx testifies in the 1848 *Manifesto of the Communist Party*, is **the history of man's oppression by man**, that is, of his constant *alienation*. There is therefore only one way to recover man's natural *identity*, insofar as man possesses a primary identity, as Rousseau saw it as God's creation: to break with this prehistory of humanity and begin a new history. **To put it plainly, the revolution wants to put an end to the old man, whether dominant or dominated, and create a new one.**

But how to create it with old men, even when they claim to be revolutionaries? French revolutionaries, like those in Russia and elsewhere, did not escape the **trap** of **a revolution that devours its own children**. In 1793, the Comité de salut public, with Billaud-Varenne and Collot d'Herbois, instituted a Terror that executed a hundred thousand people, including the instigators and supporters of the massacres. Hegel would not hesitate to say, with the French Revolution in mind, that absolute Freedom equals absolute Terror. Camus, who was severe about the denial of freedom embodied in the revolution, underlined the paradox in his *Carnets* (V, 1945): **"The human effort towards freedom and its *usual* contradiction: discipline and freedom die by their own hand."** Understandably, Marxists in the 1950s, like their progressive allies, condemned this condemnation of revolution in favor of revolt.

Camus could then assert, against the illusions of the revolution that wants to start history from scratch, that **"the world always ends up defeating history"** (*L'Été*, 1939). It's as if the world, with its stability and serenity, were an example of measure for man confronted with the excesses of history. But, in the final analysis, it is indeed the world, which we enter through the door of birth, that establishes in man this model of an eternal order impossible to violate without being punished by the gods, or by the world itself, which brings death. Revolution is therefore a challenge from history, **as if it too wanted to bring death to those who do not accept its violence.** In *The Rebel*, Camus quotes two revolutionary declarations that are truly

«LE MONDE FINIT TOUJOURS
PAR VAINCRE L'HISTOIRE»

revolting. That of Saint-Just, who approved the guillotine with his terrible "no one can reign innocently", and that of Marat, even more cynical, who said of the opponents of the Revolution: "Brand them with a hot iron, cut off their thumbs, slit their tongues." We know what happened to Marat, murdered in his bathtub, and Saint-Just, guillotined at the age of twenty-six.

How, then, to think about the course of history and the political model that would be the right measure of humanity? Camus harbored a deep distrust of power, as demonstrated in his plays, particularly *Caligula* and *The Just*. What drives all power, even if it is dedicated to freedom like revolution, is **its exasperation, which, in seeking to surpass itself, leads it towards its own end and, sometimes, its own death.** We are reminded of the words of Lord Acton, the great English liberal thinker: "Power tends to corrupt, absolute power corrupts absolutely." To limit power, if not abolish it, Camus opts for authority. In the preparatory notes for *The First Man*, we find this brief note: **"Authority, not power"**. Although Camus never deals explicitly with authority, as Hannah Arendt would lament its disappearance in the modern world, he makes the search for the Father the model for the search for Authority. **In the final analysis,**

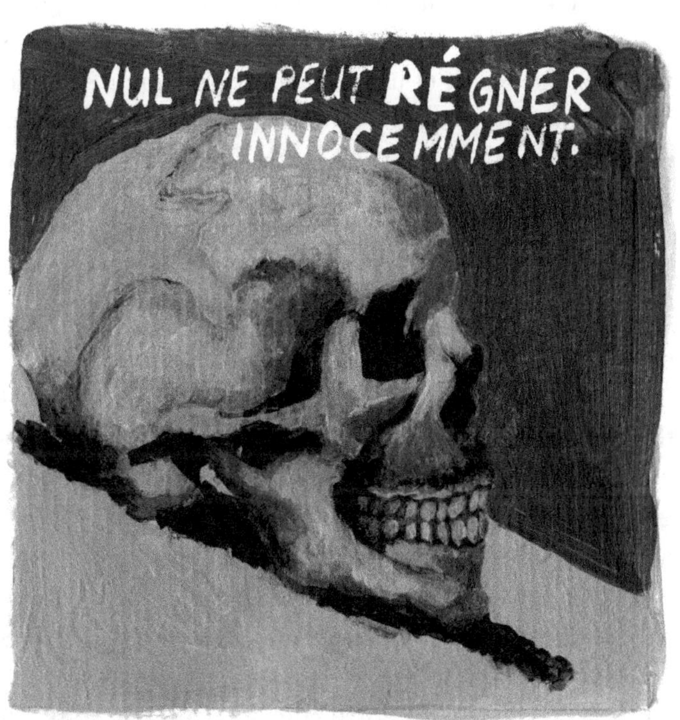
NUL NE PEUT RÉGNER
INNOCEMMENT.

there is no true authority except that of the father, who teaches the son to become a man. This is why the first part of *The First Man* is entitled "Search for the Father". Camus senses that, in the absence of a father whose grave he will have known only, every man seeks that *auctoritas* which enables each of us to *increase,* in Latin *augere,* our possibilities of existence. **The authority of the father who gave him birth merges with the authority of the teacher who gave him knowledge.**

Camus refused to accept this as the authority of history. This choice kept him away from the progressive movements of his time, first and foremost the Marxists. It could even be said that this is **what radically distinguishes him from the Moderns and places him on the side of the Ancients: he does not believe in the ever-changing movements of history, but in the unchanging presence of the world.** And if he doesn't believe in history, which has claimed to be rational since Hegel and Marx, it's because he doesn't believe in the empire of reason. He asserts his difference with his contemporaries in a text from *L'Été,* "Les Amandiers": **"I don't believe enough in reason to subscribe to progress, nor do I believe in any philosophy of history."** The question is clear-cut. Whereas the entire philosophical tradition, at least since Descartes, has relied on rationalism as a system, to the point of seeing it, along with the Enlighten-ment, as the justification for history, Camus rejects reason, progress and history with the same skepticism. How can we believe in the **new providence that is the history of reason** when, in the 20th century, we see the same injustices and horrors being repeated with the help of science and technology? While the world turns in on itself, unchanging but innocent, history moves forward, shifting and always guilty.

The rejection of progress—all the more surprising given that the Left, and not just Marxism as it then prevailed, declared itself progressive by opposing "reactionaries" who didn't subscribe to it—was a constant feature of Camus's thinking and sensibility. In one of his first articles on "Indigenous culture", written for the Algerian magazine *Jeune Méditerranée* in April 1937, Camus declared that "it would be too dangerous to handle this evil toy called progress". **He had joined the Communist Party in 1935 and, during his formative years, was active in the theater and journalism unions**. But while he remained faithful to his libertarian trade union commit-ments, he never wavered in his distrust of progress. It's not just a reassuring illusion that history engenders, and that reality denounces, it's an **evil toy**. A toy, and the term is well chosen, because it concerns adults who have remained children, a childishness therefore; evil, and the condemnation is definitive, because it perverts the good intentions of those who believed in the legitimacy of revolt. But you don't have to believe in progress to revolt! Revolt in the face of injustice, as exemplified by the tragedy that will always haunt Camus, can be found in Sophocles, Shakespeare and Racine, in eras that ignored both progress and progressism.

We can understand the reluctance, and even more the **condemnation, of any revolution for someone who believed only in revolt.** If revolt is driven by the affirmation of justice, revolution betrays its initial impulse by obeying the negation of reality. **Camus borrowed the term *nihilism* from Nietzsche to denounce the fascination with nothingness** that has often seduced intellectuals, and sometimes artists, in their desire to annihilate all that is established, men and works alike. We see this in his adaptation of Dostoyevsky's *Demons* or in *The Just*, the tragedies that strike down the most ardent revolutionaries, driven by Nemesis. After Camus's death, Sartre would not hesitate to continue celebrating the revolution, to the point of declaring in *Actuel* magazine in 1972: "The revolutionaries of 1793 probably didn't kill enough." **How could Camus not have been revolted by this one-upmanship of the guillotine?**

He gradually but definitively separated himself from the progressive circles that attacked him violently when *The Rebel* was published. **The criticism in *Les Temps modernes*, led by Francis Jeanson in his virulent May 1952 article, "Albert Camus ou l'âme révoltée", marked Camus's final divorce from his former friends.** Less well known is his two-part reply to the attacks of Emmanuel d'Astier de la Vigerie, a fellow Communist from the aristocracy. Camus curtly reminded him that the vast majority of **"communist intellectuals" had "no personal experience of the proletarian condition".** Whereas the man they were attacking in the name of history, Astier even calling him "Pontius Pilate", had been born into a miserable environment and had managed, through study and willpower, not money or the bourgeoisie, to escape it. We need to go even further. What Camus reproached the left-wingers of his time, whether communists, socialists or progressives, was that they **only became indignant with their adversaries at "fixed times and in one direction only".** Emmanuel Mounier, for example, although a Christian philosopher and creator of personalism, had no hesitation in speaking out against those, like Arthur Koestler, who dared to criticize the "positive work of the Communist Party". And, to weaken the horror, he identified the Soviet concentration camps with the working-class suburbs of Paris (*Esprit*, February 1950).

It wasn't Camus who abandoned the universal moral positions of the Left; it was, in his eyes, the Left that abandoned those moral positions to which the whole of humanity belongs. When Camus was asked to take a position on the Hungarian revolution of October 1956, he noted that **many left-wing intellectuals, and not just Communists, did not condemn the terrible Soviet repression** that ended with the hanging of Imre Nagy. Not content with noting, with irony, that the usual revolutionaries had become "hemiplegic", he also pointed out that "conformism today is on the left" ("Le socialisme des potences", *Demain*, no. 63, 1957). **From his earliest political commitments until his death, Camus remained at odds** with the left, despite the fact that it was his natural milieu. Whether on the USSR and its satellite countries, the Soviet camps, Israel or Algeria, he rejected a "schizophrenic left" that failed to put its humanitarian ideals into practice, the better to challenge his opponents on the right.

Always faithful to the balancing act between refusal and consent, negation and affirmation which, in politics, take the form of left and right, Camus rejected **the substantive existence of a left frozen in its progressivism and**

« SI, ENFIN, LA VÉRITÉ ME PARAISSAIT
À DROITE, J'Y SERAIS »

a right paralyzed in its conservatism. In his famous reply to *Les Temps modernes* in June 1952, he refused to reduce the "truth of a thought" to its position on the right or left, and even less to what men on the right and those on the left decide to do with it by manipulating that truth. And he didn't hesitate to defy the conformism of *Les Temps modernes*, Jean-Paul Sartre's magazine, by concluding: **"If, at last, truth seemed to me to be on the right, I'd be there."** We are reminded of Aristotle's words in the *Nicomachean* Ethics (I, 4): "Truth and friendship are both dear to us, but it is our sacred duty to give preference to truth."

V - Drama of Algeria

Algeria was a tragedy for France and the French after the FLN's armed insurrection on November 1, 1954, which became known as the "Red All Saints Day". For the French in metropolitan France knew nothing about a country they believed to be an African colony inhabited by unscrupulous colonists, when in fact it consisted of **three departments that had become French in 1858 before the annexation of the county of Nice and Savoie two years later.** Apart from the Arab and Kabyle peoples, the vast majority of the population of Algeria was made up of modest Europeans of all origins—Alsatians, Provençals, Maltese, Spaniards, Corsicans, Italians and Jews—whose income was far lower than that of the French on the mainland. The latter had little sympathy for their compatriots from the southern Mediterranean, whom they called "Algerians" before referring to them as "pieds-noirs" (black feet) and disassociating themselves from them during the events in Algeria, which the state authorities refused to call the "Algerian War".

ALGERIE

For Camus, this was more than a tragedy, it was a personal tragedy. He had been one of the first intellectuals, both in Algeria and in France, **to reveal the misery of part of the Muslim world, especially in Kabylia.** As early as the 1930s, he had written a "Manifesto of Algerian intellectuals" in the magazine *Jeune Méditerranée* (1937), after having investigated in the *bled*, at a time when no intellectuals in metropolitan France were interested in Algeria and even less in Algerians. **His *Chroniques algériennes*, published regularly from 1939 to 1958,** demonstrated his concern for justice and his support for the demands of Arab nationalists. But as soon as the war escalated and left-wing intellectuals, relying on the indifference and then hostility of metropolitan France towards a war that threatened the lives of their children, took a stand in favor of Algerian independence, Camus was rejected by his milieu. **His attachment to his homeland was so strongly criticized, especially by the Sartrians (Simone de Beauvoir in particular),** that he wrote the following decisive remark in *The First Man*: "**What they didn't like about him was the Algerian.**"

The misunderstanding was never cleared up, and was reinforced by a new misunderstanding between Camus and the French in Algeria, who accused him of being a "liberal" in favor of independence. A stranger among his own people both in Paris and Algiers, Camus devoted all his energies as a journalist and writer to dispelling the doubts. He called on history, which he distrusted, to rectify the false image metropolitans had of a world unknown to them. This was the project behind *The First Man,* which would have been, had the author not died in a car accident on January 4, 1960, the novel of the French presence in Algeria. Camus was as attached to his native Algeria as he was to the French culture that had lifted him out of poverty. The posthumous novel *The First Man* was intended to convert all **"French values into an Algerian consciousness"**. The story features a man, Jacques Cormery, who is Camus's double, as we shall see, and who would have been the "First Man", the one who, on the basis of the culture he has received from the past, can open wide the doors to the future and to creation, **as if all humanity were beginning anew with him**.

But to justify this new beginning, which would have created an original culture in Algeria based on the old Mediterranean, it was necessary to respect all the peoples living on the same land, first and foremost the Arabs and the Kabyles. When Camus wrote in 1945, at the end of the war, when people were more interested in the desolation of Europe than in the poverty of Algeria, that "the Arab people exists" and cannot be reduced to an "anonymous and miserable

DISSIPER
LES DOUTES

crowd" ("Crise en Algérie", *Actuelles III*), **he was one of the few writers to feel responsible for the fate of the Algerians and their unrecognized culture.** From then on—and Camus's words are harsh on France, while leaving it some hope—the only excuse for the "colonial conquest" of 1830, which cannot be reversed because history has imposed its course, is to help "the conquered peoples to retain their personality" ("Misère de la Kabylie", *Actuelles III*).

Camus' dilemma must be understood. His loyalty was twofold: to the country of his birth—father and mother united in the same love, an impossible love since the father was dead and the mother diminished—and to the country of his upbringing—French culture and, through it, the great European culture. He could sacrifice neither without sacrificing himself on the altar of ideology. **His father was a simple farm worker and his mother a deaf, illiterate cleaning lady.** We're a long way from the epinal image of the colonist exploiting the Algerians. If colonization had committed crimes against the natives, and Camus recognized this, we couldn't erase at a stroke the benefits of a culture that balanced the misdeeds of the colony. The equivocation is all the greater in that **the French words *culture* and *colonie* derive from the same Latin verb *colere*, which gave *cultura* and *colonia*,** the care given to the *cultivation of* a piece of

«CETTE PATRIE N'EXISTE PAS»

land or a man, and to the *colony* that the *cultivator, i.*e. the *colonist*, works to extract its fruits.

Camus didn't rely on sentiment alone to defend Algeria's attachment to France. He had solid historical arguments, which some Algerian independence fighters had recognized. The nationalist leader Ferhat Abbas, vice-president of the UNEF in 1930 and later a pharmacist, had published a "Manifesto of the Algerian people" in 1943, in which he called for a new status for Algeria. But before joining the FLN in 1955, he had written in *L'Entente in* 1936: "I won't die for the Algerian homeland because it doesn't exist. I have questioned the living and the dead, I have visited cemeteries: no one has spoken to me about it." Camus replied to him point-blank in "Algérie 1958" (*Actuelles III*): **"There has never yet been an Algerian nation. The Jews, Turks, Greeks, Italians and Berbers would have just as much right to claim leadership of this virtual nation."** Indeed, since ancient times, the Maghreb had been subjected to a tidal wave of settlements and colonizations, from the Phoenicians, Jews and Romans to the Vandals, the Arabs, who imposed their language and religion on the Berbers, the Spanish, and finally the Ottomans, who put a dey at the head of the regency of Algiers until the French conquest in 1830, who gave the country the name of Algeria.

As a result, in Camus' eyes, the French presence in Algeria, more deeply rooted than in Morocco and Tunisia—which were protectorates rather than departments—was justified by **the presence of over a million Europeans and by the French culture that had transformed the country**. In a famous letter to an Algerian militant, Aziz Kessous, on October 1, 1955, Camus forcefully asserted that "the 'French fact' cannot be eliminated in Algeria", to the point that "the dream of a sudden disappearance of France is childish". And he was wrong: puerile or not, the dream turned into a nightmare in 1962, when almost a million pieds-noirs hurriedly left their homes and lands to take refuge in a France most of them had never known. Communities of European origin—Alsatians, Lorrains, Corsicans and Provençals, Spaniards, Maltese, Greeks and Germans—as well as the many Sephardic Jews who had settled in Algeria since Roman times, had lived for generations on the same land as the Berbers and Arabs. They had worked and transformed much of the country, bringing with them all the technical innovations of Europe: roads, railroads, electricity, industry and, above all, the reclamation of the Mitidja farmlands and the draining of the swamps. Camus feared that these achievements would be dissipated by independence, and that the disappearance of France would turn Algeria into a "land of ruins and death" (*Letter to Aziz Kessous*).

« une terre de
ruines
et de morts »

What did Camus propose? Despite his notoriety, he was neither understood nor heard by the Algerian independence fighters, by the Parisian progressives of the Jeanson network who were the FLN's "bag carriers", and also by his fellow Europeans, most of whom reproached him for his links with the independence fighters. Camus, as always, took a measured stance. **He expected the belligerents to agree to a new Algeria made up of "federated peoples"**, linked to France by legal, economic and cultural ties, and not to an "Islamic empire" that would plunge the Arab peoples of the Mediterranean into "added misery and suffering" ("Chroniques algériennes", *Actuelles III*, 1958). Far from selfishly supporting a French presence indifferent to the poverty of the natives, Camus wanted to grant all populations the same rights associated with the progress of modernity, by rooting them in the continuity of Mediterranean culture. In *Actuelles III*, his last book published before his death, he rejected the idea that Algeria should lose its European component, which had been part of the country for over a century, and become part of an Islamic world that would take over from the Ottoman Empire. **It was not France that would suffer from the loss of Algeria, which it was carrying economically at arm's length, but Algeria itself, which risked being bogged down in civil war and poverty.**

Camus refused, right up to the end, on the one hand to blame France, and then Europe, for the misdeeds of a colonialism that had been practiced by all peoples, and which, in Algeria, had brought economic, social and cultural benefits; on the other hand, to "beat one's bosom"—we would say "do penance" today, but "beat one's bosom on the bosom of others", in the image of the penitent Judge Clamence in *The Fall*. Once again, the decisive break with the anti-colonialist left, which had been so enraged by Europe's expansion since 1492 that, as Camus explains in *Actuelles III*, it **"included Christopher Columbus and Lyautey in the same curse"**. Marshal Lyautey, who became Morocco's first resident general in 1912, protected Moroccan culture, particularly the traditional centers of the medinas, while admiring the pride and religious convictions of the Moroccan people. Out of respect for real people and their beliefs, Camus could not accept that **the humanist heritage of France and Europe should be denied with a stroke of the pen, or a burst of bombs**, by ideo logists or terrorists who, while claiming to fight the battles of history, claimed to dispense with its lessons.

This can be seen in the exchange of letters with the poet Jean Sénac, an Algerian like Camus. **Sénac was a fervent supporter of the FLN who criticized his**

friend's measured stance on the Algerian conflict. Accused of hypocrisy, Camus replied to Sénac that he had not varied in his defense of justice. He questioned the FLN's attacks, which killed more Muslims than Europeans, and generalized the use of terrorism against civilians rather than war against the military. **Sénac was indifferent to the independence fighters' bombs thrown into cafés or streets, indiscriminately killing innocent bystanders, and maintained, in defense of the terrorists, that the French were as criminal as they were.** But Camus noticed a difference: on the French side, men like him and Sénac had defended the natives and criticized the excesses of colonialism. But on the side of the Algerian independence fighters, no one condemned the terrorist attacks or the **massacres of Muslims like the one in the douar of Melouza on May 29, 1957.** In one night, the three hundred and fifteen inhabitants of a village were killed with knives, pickaxes and machine guns, then mutilated by the FLN. Camus concludes his letter by saying that, today as yesterday, he absolutely condemns the "murder of innocent civilians".

VI - Gift of Love

THE THIRD AND FINAL CYCLE OF CAMUS' WORK WAS SUPPOSED TO BE THAT OF LOVE. Barely begun with *The First Man*, which remained unfinished, it actually commands the first two cycles of the absurd and revolt. Camus had placed it under the sign of Nemesis. **The Greek goddess derives her name from the verb *nemein*, "to share", and the noun *nomos*, "law".** She is thus the cosmic principle that fairly distributes the fates of all and compensates for the wrongs of unjust sharing. Camus uses this mythical figure to illustrate not only the inescapability of justice, but also the power of love. It's as if the writer from Algiers identified justice not with the vengeance of society, but with the love of world order, embodied from the outset in maternity.

It is his mother who, in the strangeness of her silence, evokes for Camus the distance from Nemesis and the love she bears for justice. The sole source of his entire work, as he has repeatedly said, is to be found in the five essays of his first book, *The Wrong Side and the Right Side*:

"L'ironie", "Entre oui et non", "La mort dans l'âme", "Amour de vivre" and "L'Envers et l'Endroit". All revolve around the figure of the mother, whose silence has not restored the son's love for her. Camus places at the center of his search **"the admirable silence of a mother and the effort of a man to find a justice or a love that balances this silence"** (late preface to *The Wrong Side and the Right Side,* 1958, two years before his death). The mother was unable to bring to the son a love that remained buried beneath the failure of the spoken word; he then entrusted to the respect of writing the love that he carried without hope to his mother, and, through her, to the world.

The First Man, who questions the enigma of his origin, precisely because he knows, like other men, that he *came into the world* from a man and a woman, starts from the search for the father to arrive at the discovery of the mother. These two faces of the same origin are both absent for Camus: **so he feels alienated from other men who have known the love of a father and a mother**. All he sees of his father is the tomb in Saint-Brieuc, and all he hears of his mother is her near-silence. The absurdity of his existence bursts forth in the measure of his impossible love. **He admits in his novel that what he wanted most of all was for "his mother to read everything that was his life and his flesh"**: but, illiterate as she

le premier Homme

was, she was incapable of reading a line of her son's: what would she have understood of the plot of *The First Man*? And yet, while the book opens with the birth of Albert Camus and immediately sets off on the "Search for the Father", it is dedicated to his mother, "you who will never be able to read this book". Camus experienced in his flesh and soul the absurd powerlessness of not being able to express his love for the woman who had given him life. **He breaks this religious silence with a mystical prayer to his mother, which takes on a Christ-like quality**: "O Mother, forgive your son for having fled the night of your truth."

For a Christian, "God is love, and he who abides in love abides in God, and God abides in him" (First Letter of John, 4:16). Camus is not a Christian, and places love not in God, but in Nemesis. **Yet the figure of the mother brings him back to Christianity, that** is, to the Son. That's why we read this astonishing sentence in *The First Man*: **"His mother *is* Christ."** And if it's true that the Son identifies with the mother, then Camus, without going so far as to sign his letters, like the last Nietzsche, "le Crucifié", does indeed identify with Christ. A Christ who says to his mother: "Why have you forsaken me?" like Jesus says to his Father. **Camus has always been fascinated by Pascal, and the sense of dereliction that**

Pascal discovers in the misfortune of man without God; but through Pascal, it's the figure of Jesus that fascinates him. Jesus is not God for him, just as Prince Muishkin is not Christ for Dostoyevsky. Nevertheless, reading Dostoyevsky and Camus, the reader understands that both writers identify, one with his character, the other with his mother, with the passion of Christ. Camus, the unbeliever, would not hesitate to say of his mother, again in the unfinished novel: "May the cross sustain her!"

His religious love for his mother justified Camus's political and polemical choice of justice in the Algerian affair. It was Nemesis, too, who taught him true fairness in his outcry against terrorism. **In Greece, Nemesis is the figure of justice violated, and therefore of the divine indignation that will restore world order**. After receiving the Nobel Prize for Literature on December 10, 1957, Camus was invited to speak to students in Stockholm two days later. There was a polemic between Camus and a young Algerian who strongly criticized him for not signing petitions in support of the FLN, even though he had defended the peoples of Eastern Europe under the Communist yoke. Camus recalled that he had always condemned terror, wherever it came from, and developed his conception of justice, which was recalled by a journalist from *Le Monde* in a condensed and incorrect form:

"I believe in justice, but I will defend my mother before justice."

The very next day, and for years to come, the phrase caused a scandal in left-wing circles, which interpreted it as a particular preference for an individual, perhaps a mother, to the detriment of the universality of justice. Camus would have departed from the requirement of rationality and thus revealed his support for the ultras of French Algeria by choosing the side of colonialism. Simone de Beauvoir was particularly virulent, concluding without further ado in *La Force des choses* that **Camus was "on the side of the pieds-noirs"**. The reality was quite different. Camus's exact quote, which was reinstated too late, was as follows: **"At the moment, bombs are being thrown into the streetcars of Algiers. My mother could be on one of those streetcars. If that's justice, I prefer my mother."** Camus was condemning terrorism against the civilian population of Algeria, just as he had condemned the dropping of the atomic bomb on the civilian populations of Hiroshima and Nagasaki. Crimes against innocent people, torn apart by bombs hidden in public places, could not be, whatever the cause of the murderers, an act of justice. **Antigone's unwritten law is always legitimate and superior to ideologies of hatred, even if they take the mask of Creon's law.**

If Nemesis embodied the mythical figure of love for Camus, it was also insofar as she symbolized the equitable sharing of justice that gives everyone their share. And this share, which is allotted to us, condenses in itself all the love in the world. In his fourth *Letter to a German friend*, Camus writes that he chose justice, not Nazi violence, "to remain faithful to the earth". **If this world has no "higher meaning", all transcendence abolished, be it religious or metaphysical,** something in us bears witness to a love for the world that gives man his dignity, for he is the only being to demand meaning. The misfortune of Europe in the thirties and forties, the Europe of Fascism, Nazism and Communism—a misfortune it dare not admit to itself, for such is its "secret"—is that "it no longer loves life" (*The Rebel*). If Camus contrasted the Mediterranean light of Algeria with the warlike night of Europe, it was because he placed the love of life, and therefore of the world, above the battle of ideologies.

In his play *The Just*, he portrays Russian terrorists seeking to assassinate the uncle of Tsar Nicholas II. The main character, **Ivan Kaliayev, a socialist poet who is to throw a bomb into Grand Duke Serge's carriage, turns away from the attack when he sees the aristocrat's wife and two nephews in the carriage.** He repeated the attempt two days later, this time killing the Grand Duke. Camus uses this historical episode to expose the dilemma of revolutionaries who are willing to kill innocent people in pursuit of their own justice. After the first failed attempt, Ivan is attacked by Stepan Fedorov, who refuses to bow to "ignoble love" in favor of the "bomb [which] is revolutionary". Once again, **we see the conflict between revolt, which raises its indignation against a backdrop of love for life, and revolution, which explodes its resentment against a backdrop of hatred for love.** It is indeed love of the world that is man's primary driving force, even before he becomes aware of the absurdity of a life against which he is going to revolt. To Stepan, who brutally declares: "A true revolutionary cannot love himself", and to Dora, who adds that "those who truly love justice have no right to love", Ivan simply replies: **"But that's what love is, giving everything, sacrificing everything with no hope of return."**

If we return to the source of Camus's work, *The Wrong Side and the Right Side*, we find two complementary texts, the first entitled "La mort dans l'âme", and the second "Amour de vivre". In the first, we see Camus wandering, as Rousseau does in *Les Rêveries*, not in Paris or Île Saint-Pierre, but in Vicenza and its Italian countryside. He discovers his wonder as he encounters people for a day or an evening. **"Every being I meet,"** he writes, **"every smell on this street, everything is a pretext for me to love without measure."** In the second short story, which contrasts the love of living with death in the soul, the author shares with us his discovery of Palma de Mallorca and Ibiza. His love of life is sharpened by this simple, "ironic and discreet" world, whose hills turn green as evening falls and the pure emotion of existing rises. Twilight whispers in a melancholy tone. And Camus confides to himself: **"For me, I wanted to love like one wants to cry."** Catherine Sintès' son had never recovered from his childhood.

His childhood and adolescence, spent in Algiers and Oran, left an indelible mark of love and justice on his life as a man. His most beautiful declaration of love, not to his mother, but to his native land, is found in the famous "Retour à Tipasa" in *L'Été* (1954). **For Camus, it's all about meeting his first love in the early mornings of the world.** As in Proust, with the episode of the madeleine that instantly gives him back the taste of eternity that the past has given him, the episode of the ruins of Tipasa, discovered in 1939, before the war, makes Camus realize that his life will always resonate with the harmonics of the Algerian landscape mixed with Roman temples. Here, perhaps, we have the decisive sentence

« CETTE ARDEUR ET CETTE LUMIÈRE »

that illuminates Camus's work: **"When one has once had the good fortune to love strongly, one's life is spent seeking again that ardor and that light."** The enigma of existence is concentrated in this double paradox. That of the contrast between the absurdity of a world whose overwhelming presence underlines the futility of a man about to disappear. And that of the noise of history, which is always the history of war and death, preventing men from living and loving in the silence of creation. Camus drew a lesson from this in "Noces à Tipasa" (*Noces*): **"I understand here what is called glory: the right to love without measure. There is only one love in this world."**

VII - God's Silence

Camus' thought, punctuated by the cycles of the absurd, revolt and love, obeys a higher sphere that encompasses all three, the sphere of existence. Like Nietzsche's eternal return, this sphere turns the three cycles back on themselves. Love, already present in the denunciation of the absurd in order to justify it, finds itself once again in the permanence of the absurd in order to overcome it. What is the mark, and therefore the reality, of absurd sentiment? The ineradicable belief in the presence of meaning within the disorder of the world, which man tries to reproduce in history, and the equally irrefutable observation that there is none. **This absence, which leaves us waiting for the coming of a hidden presence, is that of God**. All religions call upon a God or gods to guide human actions and judge them, but none, for Camus, succeeds in assuring believers, and even more so unbelievers, of the reality of this invisible being. Pascal, who so influenced Camus, spoke of the ***deus abscon-***

ditus, the **"hidden God"**, drawing on Isaiah's text in the Bible (XLV, 15): "You are truly the god who hides himself, the god of Israel, the Savior."

As I said earlier, the other great inspiration for Camus was Dostoyevsky. In most of his works, the Russian novelist presents characters who suffer to the point of suicide from the absence of God. Kirilov, for example, in *Demons*, which Camus adapted for the stage under the title *The Possessed* and analyzed in *The Myth of Sisyphus*, asserts that if God does not exist, he himself is God. **But since he has identified himself with the absence of God, he must kill himself to truly be God**. In metaphysical terms, s yllogism is tantamount to arguing that if there is no being, there is only nothingness. But since nothingness *is* the being it denies, it must therefore *deny itself* to truly be being. Camus concludes: "This logic is absurd, but it's what's necessary." **Why is it necessary? Because** man lives in what Camus, in the same text from *The Myth of Sisyphus*, calls the "hell of the present". Here we find the first mention of the circles of hell that will be evoked in *The Fall*. **The present is *hell* insofar as, if God doesn't exist and man is alone in the universe, no one can give *meaning* to the time that imperturbably unrolls its rings**. Time reproduces the emptiness of becoming, old age and death, over which man has no control. Even if he commits suicide to avoid this confinement in the dungeon of existence, he is merely anticipating his own impending death.

So we'll never get out of the Platonic cave, except by dream or illusion, and Socrates himself ended his myth with the prisoner returning to the cave to die. Kirilov is Camus' mask when he says, in the play: **"All my life, I've been tormented by God."** The confession comes from Dostoyevsky himself, who put it into his character's mouth. But it can also be seen as Camus' confession: to be tormented by God is to be tormented by an absence that signals, in a hollow way, a possible presence whose subtraction we do not understand. It's all the more difficult to understand because, **in the total absence of God, for the believer, or in the total absence of being, for the philosopher, nothing makes sense**. There is no justice unless a "supreme master" (*Oberhaupt*), as Kant put it, establishes the universal norms of a reign of ends. But there is no reality if a hidden being does not guarantee the universal stability of appearances. In the absence of God, would everything be permitted—evil and all its variations? In the absence of being, would everything be temporary, appearance and its illusions?

The proven existence of evil in the world raises not the problem of man, but the question of God. **How is evil**

possible? This is the source of all ethical reflection and, dare I say it, the philosophers' "cross". For if God does not exist, how can we understand the presence of evil and man's inability to overcome it, unless we assume that man is naturally evil? **But if God does exist—and the idea of God includes from the outset the goodness of man, whom he created in his own image—why does he allow evil to exist, and why does he deliver innocent children to suffering?** I showed this with the death of the young patient in *The Plague*, which outrages Dr. Rieux, who could do nothing with his remedies, any more than Father Paneloux could with his prayers. According to Jean Sarocchi, when Camus wrote *The Plague* in Oran, where he was staying with friends, he didn't come to the table one evening to worry the lady of the house. She found him distraught in his room, the writer repeating over and over again about the sick child in his novel: **"I've just made a child die. I killed a child and he was screaming to die!"** He asked his hostess to hold his hand for most of the night, and spoke of the poverty he had known as a child. The young woman kept him this way until morning, when he finally dozed off after asking her, **"Can one be a saint without God?"**

« IL CRIAIT POUR MOURIR »

Was Camus then a *lay* saint and not a *religious one*? We know that he was agnostic, and that he didn't believe in God any more than he believed in the divinity of Jesus. What would have become of him if the car accident hadn't turned his life and work into a destiny? Some interpreters have speculated that he might have had a conversion, as lightning-fast as Paul Claudel's on December 25, 1886 at Notre-Dame de Paris. **We don't know, and the nature of conversion is precisely that it cannot be predicted.** We can, however, highlight Camus's ethical concern, which often takes on a Christian form in his insistence on love as the supreme stage of existence. Yet it was Christianity that conceived of a God made man entirely devoted to love, to the extent that Jesus Christ gave his life for the love of humanity. It is undoubtedly this sacrifice that Camus, following Nietzsche, cannot rationally accept: how can we understand, if not by the faith of a conversion, that God sacrifices himself to save his creatures in the way a creditor would commit suicide to help his debtors?

The question of evil, however, remains unanswered. We see this in *Letters to a German Friend,* in which Camus ponders the criminal choices of Nazism in 1945, when he was still unaware of the extermination camps of the Shoah. Like his "German friend", a term charged with chilling irony, Camus believes that there is no "higher reason" for man to dictate his actions, and that the world is devoid of God. Like Pascal's libertine, man finds himself alone in an infinite universe devoid of meaning. But Nazi ideology has drawn a perverse conclusion from this: if there is no transcendent authority to forbid certain acts, nothing is superior to nothing, which amounts to saying, writes Camus, that **"everything is equivalent"**: the cult of the *Fürher* and the death of the Jews, the German culture of Goethe and that of Goebbels, the murder of the prisoners of Auschwitz and the death of Don Giovanni in Mozart's opera. But Hitler's prestige should not be confused with the statue of the Commander. **"Good and Evil," concludes Camu s, "are not defined according to one's fantasy or folly."**

But then, if Camus believes neither in God nor in History, neither in Progress nor in Revolution, while remaining skeptical about the indignation of "beautiful souls", what is the authority that tells us what is good and what is evil, and enables man—the man of flesh and blood and not the abstract being of Humanism—to lead a just life? The answer lies in his graduate diploma in philosophy, defended in Algiers in 1936, *Christian Metaphysics and Neoplatonism*. At the same time, the young man studied the religious revelation of God to Saint Augustine and Plotinus' philosophical conversion to the One. Camus was, and always will be, on the side of Plotinus. For the Alexandrian thinker, the human soul was "longing for God and nostalgia for a lost homeland", that of the **"One" or "Father"**, who remains ever absent, no matter how much we *convert*, or epistrophize, towards Him. Let me remind you once again that Camus was deprived of a father, and that his absence pervades all his work, in particular *The First Man*, which had no father because it is the ***first man***, but which has a destiny of paternity because man must beget a son.

Before Hannah Arendt, Camus sensed that the fundamental category of existence is that of *natality*. This is the very mystery of life and the world: why is there man and not nothing? And it is in the enigma of *birth*, which Camus relates to both the dead father and the absent mother, that he sees the source of action and its justification. In his study of Plotinus' thought, he first uses the metaphor of the "upside and downside" of things, the title of his first book, which he calls his matrix work. The presence of the mother is constant. **In Plotinus, Camus finds the search for "the other side of things, which is his lost paradise". This was to be the common thread running through his life and work, from *The Wrong Side and the Right Side* (1937) to *Exile and the Kingdom* (1957).** When, in August 1947, Camus discovered his father's grave in Saint-Brieuc, he wrote that "death brings him back to his true homeland", as if the death of the Father were at the same time the death of God, this double death being necessary for Camus, like Plotinus, to return to his "true homeland", which is that of the earth where he was born, "under the light of the first mornings of the world".

Camus remains Plotinian, not by identifying the One with God, but by identifying the One with his homeland, the native land, this "lost paradise" being that "place where the heart will find its accord" (*Noces*). If he is constantly nostalgic for Algeria, in which nostalgia for the return to father and mother merges, it's because nostalgia is the call of the world, in its unity, to the one who comes to be through birth. This explains the first scene of *The First Man*. **It's a true Christian nativity without Christianity**. An old Arab is driving a cart containing a man and a woman on an autumn night in 1913, towards an Algerian village. The woman is about to give birth, and the vehicle stops in front of the Arab's little house. The man, a Frenchman, goes for help and sends for a doctor. In the meantime, the owner of a nearby canteen has gone to the woman in labor and helped her give birth to a boy. **He will be named Jacques Cormery in the novel, and this character is Albert Camus's double**. The father leaves the room to let the doctor cut the cord and assist the mother; he finds the old Arab who has lent him his house in the rain, and tells him it's a boy. "God be praised. You're a boss," replies the Arab.

This opening chapter of the first part of the novel, "Searching for the Father", is an imitation of the nativity of Jesus in a *manger*—Camus calls on the owner of a *canteen to* deliver his mother—in front of modest Arabs who, by contrast, recall the Magi. The father and mother are poor, like Joseph and Mary. However, the child, Jacques Cormery, will not be God, but, to use the expression Jesus used to introduce himself to his own people, the "Son of Man". **And to identify this new nativity in which "the First Man" appears, Camus gives his character, Jacques Cormery, the initials of Jesus Christ.** Readers can interpret the night of Camus's birth as "that night full of signs and stars" spoken of by Meursault at the end of *The Stranger*. He is no more Jacques Cormery than he is Jesus Christ. But he is close to Albert Camus when he turns away from God to open himself up to the "tender indifference of the world".

MEURSAULT FORMERY
CAMUS

Conclusion - The Midi of Thought

Camus may not believe in God or history, but he places all his trust in **the order of the world**, an expression he uses on several occasions. This is a Stoic and, more generally, Greek trait, which he makes the most of when he speaks, after Nietzsche's "Grand Midi" and Valéry's "Midi le juste", of the "Thought of Midi". He devotes the last part of *The Rebel* to it, as well as two miniatures of prose poetry, *Noces* and *L'Été,* among other texts. Faithful to Nemesis, who forbids men to cross the limits that define everything, and the world itself, Camus proposes a **thought of measure** that finds its model in the cosmic balance of sky and earth, shadow and sun, day and night, in a series of balances between antagonistic forces. **Such is the cosmic justice that diffuses the harmonics of Noonday Thought**. Its origins lie in Greek poetry and myth, and above all in ancient tragedy, whose constant theme is the "limit that must not be exceeded" ("On the future of tragedy", Athens, April 29 1955). At the time of these texts, Camus was much mocked for substituting the thought of measure for the science of dialectics, just as he was criticized for substituting affirmative revolt for nihilistic revolution. The author of *The Rebel* replied that measure had nothing to do with moderation or bourgeois mediocrity, and that the Greek dialectic of Heraclitus or Plato did not overcome opposites in a false synthesis, but ensured the balance of their tensions.

La Pensée de midi is a thought of polarity, which plays on the common affirmation and negation of opposing poles, which in human terms means **balancing refusal with consent**. Europe, especially in the fratricidal wars of the 20th century, has been unable to strike a balance between what Camus, in his very first book, called "yes and no" and "upside down and right side up", or, later, "exile and kingdom". And it is always the world, whether natural or transformed by man, from the landscape to the city, that teaches the writer to combine refusal of injustice with consent to beauty. In his short story "Le Désert" (*Noces*), Camus declares that Florence and Tuscany taught him that at the heart of his "revolt" against the injustices of history lay a "consent" to the beauty of the world. There are, of course, other places where consent balances revolt like light balances shadow: Algiers, Djémila, Athens or Lourmarin, all part of the Mediterranean world, and above all, of course, Tipasa.

LE MIDI JUSTE

DES MASSES MONSTRUEUSES
ET MOLLES

Even in his early days as a journalist in Algiers, Camus sang of what he lyrically called "sea, sun and women in the light" (*Rivages* magazine). These "essential and perishable goods"—note the term *"perishable"*, which from the outset denies any credit to eternity—concerned a "being nourished by sun and sea" who was in direct opposition to the "powers of abstraction and death". Camus' distrust of history and dialectics is clear. And in this same 1938 text, we find the first and perhaps best illustration of the Pensée de midi: **"a thought inspired by the play of the sun and the sea"**. In the first half of the 20th century, when the intellectual world had not yet sacrificed itself to the abstraction of structuralism and analytic philosophy, these lines by Camus were already quite incongruous. When a philosopher like Sartre, still ignorant of dialectical reason, ventured to speak of nature, it was to describe **the nausea that the sight of a chestnut root gave Roquentin**. And in *La Nausée* (1938), a year before the publication of *Noces*, Sartre speaks of a world of things that for him are reduced to "monstrous, limp masses, in disorder—naked, with a frightening, obscene nudity". Where Camus sees the very blossoming of meaning in the gush of nature, Sartre intellectualizes his mal de vivre, calling "Absurdity"—with a capital letter—"that long, dead snake" that is the root of the tree. **For him, the world is not an essential, perishable good; it is the very,**

and permanent, obscenity of a life that measures its contingency by the demesne of its nausea.

Nausea, for Sartre, is the sign of visceral rejection of a world deprived of meaning and left to chance; joy, for Camus, is the expression of loving consent to a world deprived of God, where man can overcome his exile. The masterly text in which Camus delivers the Greek background to the Pensée de midi is "L'exil d'Hélène" in *L'Été*. The author does not use Ulysses as a symbol of man's exile from his native land, even though he repeatedly identifies himself with the king of Ithaca. Instead, he chooses the queen of Sparta, Helen, who had abandoned her husband to follow Paris to Asia Minor, triggering the Trojan War. **So it was a woman, the most beautiful according to the gods, who paradoxically embodied the Greek measure that is always linked—and this justifies Camus' choice—to human excess.** In this essay, Camus salutes the "solar tragedy" of the Mediterranean, which the unbridled rationality of Europe has forgotten in its conquest of totality. In spite of Nemesis, **scientific and technical reason has violated the limits of man and the world to sink into excess.** In the aftermath of the Second World War, our exclusive reason has created a vacuum within us and around us, so that "we are completing our empire on a desert". Here, Camus recalls

Nietzsche's prophecy of the desert that is growing in the modern world: "Woe to him who harbors deserts."

"From desert to desert, we no longer find landscapes in European literature," says Camus, underlining the loss of a cosmic sense that is rarely echoed in Faulkner or Giono. And the disappearance of the landscape, Camus might have added, has been the counterpart of the disappearance of the face in abstract painting. It's as if Europe, and the world it has swept along with it, from America to Japan, has given itself over to such a debauchery of reason, and therefore of unreason, that it can no longer do without ethical and artistic transgression. "L'exil d'Hélène" seeks to re-establish the lost kingdom. And this return from exile will take place in five stages, each one a step on the road to wisdom. "Acknowledged ignorance, refusal of fanaticism, the limits of the world and of man, the beloved face, beauty at last, here is the camp where we will join the Greeks." At each of these stages, man will approach this Greek measure that exalts the order of the world, just as Helen's beauty exalts the order of love.

In contrast to the ruins of Europe, Camus returned to those of Tipasa in 1952. **He had visited the Berber village in 1935, and was intoxicated by the gods of spring and the scent of absinthe**. The deep blue sky flickered above him, giving him his first taste of "life with a taste of hot stone". On his return to one of the places of his youth, after a day of torrential rain, he delves into his past and understands that first love leads a man's life in search of the same light. This essay is a Platonic hymn to light, with several instances that seize the reader before ending with a cry of joy that is at the same time a tragic cry: "O light! This is the cry of all the characters placed, in ancient drama, before their destiny. **The cry is tragic because, as the Greeks taught us, there is no light without darkness.** Oedipus, in solving the riddle of the Sphinx, had committed an irreparable act against his parents, and had to return to the shadows by gouging out his eyes.

Tragedy is always excess, but it only achieves greatness by creating its own measure. And for Camus, this measure is always indissolubly that of art and thought. In 1942's *The Myth of Sisyphus,* Camus argued that "to think is above all to want to create a world". He took up this idea again in *The Rebel* in 1951, arguing that "the artist remakes the world on his own account". **If God didn't create the world, and if the world exists of its own accord, he nonetheless calls on man to put the finishing touches to his natural harmonies.** Aristotle said that art imitates nature and completes what nature could not. Camus agrees, seeing art as the crowning achievement of the prodigious edifice that is the world. In other words, **in the absence**

Cet édifice prodigieux

of God, the world has the first and last word, from our birth to our death. Camus's December 1957 lecture in Upsal, Sweden, on "The artist and his time" is the finest illustration of the Pensée de midi and a kind of testament to his ontology and ethics. He remains fascinated by the other side of things, for want of believing in an after-world that would double this world. The world is one, as is the being of the metaphysicians, but it constantly eludes us, even when we grasp it with pen, chisel or brush. When day turns to night, we are always nostalgic for unity:

"The world is nothing and the world is everything: this is the double, tireless cry of every true artist, the cry that keeps him upright, his eyes always open, and that, from far and wide, awakens for us in the bosom of the sleeping world the fleeting, insistent image of a reality we recognize without ever having encountered."

But before entrusting himself to the light of the North, after receiving the Nobel Prize, the writer had made the decisive confession that places Mediterranean thought in the light of the South. In the south of thought, under the bright sun of Algiers, Camus had chosen his Ithaca to reconnect with his kingdom and dispel the misunderstandings of history. If it is true that, "in the light, the world remains our first and last love", heaven and earth allow us to share its justice with other men.

Bibliography

Introduction: Misunderstanding of Thought

CAMUS (Albert), *Caligula*, followed by *Le Malentendu*, Paris, Gallimard, "Folio" series, 1972.

VALÉRY (Paul), "Le cimetière marin", *Charmes*, Paris, Gallimard, coll. "Poésie", 1983.

Chapter one: Disquieting Strangeness

"1969. Lacan à Vincennes", *Magazine littéraire spécial Lacan*, no. 121, February 1977.

The Private Journals of Edvard Munch, University of Wisconsin, 2005.

CAMUS (Albert), "Carnets", in *Œuvres complètes II et IV*, Paris, Gallimard, coll. "La Pléiade", 2006 and 2008.

DELEUZE (Gilles) and GUATTARI (Félix), *Qu'est-ce que la philosophie?* Paris, éditions de Minuit, 1991.

Chapter II: Double Game of the Absurd

BAUDELAIRE (Charles), "Mon cœur mis à nu", in *Œuvres complètes*, Paris, Robert Laffont, coll. "Bouquins", 2011.

CAMUS (Albert), *L'Envers et l'Endroit*, in *Œuvres complètes I*, Paris, Gallimard, coll. "La Pléiade", 2006; *La Peste*, in *Œuvres complètes II*, Paris, Gallimard, coll. "La Pléiade", 2006.

DOSTOYEVSKY (Fyodor), *Les Démons*, Paris, Le Livre de Poche, 2011.

HEIDEGGER (Martin), *Être et Temps*, Paris, Authentica, 1985.

PLOTINUS, *Enneads*, Paris, Flammarion, 2002-2008.

SPINOZA, *Éthique*, Paris, Gallimard, "Folio-Essais", 1994.

Chapter III: Justifying Revolt

BROCHIER (Jean-Jacques), *Albert Camus, philosophe pour classes terminales*, Paris, Balland, 1979.

CAMUS (Albert), *Lettres à un ami allemand* (1943-1945), in *Œuvres complètes II*, Paris, Gallimard, coll. "La Pléiade", 2006.

CAMUS (Albert), KOESTLER (Arthur), BLOCH-MICHEL (Jean), *Réflexions sur la peine capitale*, Paris, Calmann-Lévy, 1957.

GIDE (André), *Le Prométhée mal enchaîné*, Paris, Gallimard, 1925.

SAINT PAUL, *Epistle to the Corinthians I*, XIII, 12.

Chapter IV: Betrayal of the Revolution

ARISTOTLE, *Nicomachean Ethics*, translation by J. Tricot, Paris, Vrin, 1972.

CAMUS (Albert), *Carnets V*, in *Œuvres complètes II*, Paris, Gallimard, coll. "La Pléiade", 2006.

CAMUS (Albert), "Les Amandiers" (1940), *L'Été*, in *Œuvres complètes III*, Paris, Gallimard, coll. "La Pléiade", 2008.

JEANSON (Francis), "Albert Camus ou l'âme révoltée", *Les Temps modernes*, no. 79, May 1952.

MARX (Karl), *Manifesto of the Communist Party*, Paris, éditions sociales, 1966.

Chapter V: Drama of Algeria

CAMUS (Albert), "Manifeste des intellectuels d'Algérie", *Jeune Méditerranée* (1937), in *Œuvres complètes I*, Paris, Gallimard, coll. "La Pléiade", 2006.

CAMUS (Albert), "Misère de la Kabylie", "Crise en Algérie", "Algérie 1958", "Lettre à un militant algérien", *Actuelles III*, in *Œuvres complètes IV*, Paris, Gallimard, La Pléiade, 2008.

Camus (Albert), "Lettre à Jean Sénac" (February 10, 1957), *in* Valensi (Jacqueline), *Réflexions sur le terrorisme*, Paris, Nicolas Philippe, 2002, pp. 173-176.

Chapter VI: Gift of Love

Beauvoir (Simone de), *La Force des choses*, Paris, Gallimard, 1963.

Camus (Albert), *L'Envers et l'Endroit*, in *Œuvres complètes I*, Paris, Gallimard, coll. "La Pléiade", 2006.

Camus (Albert), *Les Justes*, in *Œuvres complètes III*, Paris, Gallimard, coll. "La Pléiade", 2008.

Chapter VII: God's Silence

Claudel (Paul), "Ma conversion", in *Œuvres en prose*, Paris, Gallimard, coll. "La Pléiade", 1965.

Kant (Emmanuel), *Fondements de la métaphysique des mœurs*, translation from the German by Victor Delbos revised by A. Philonenko, Paris, Vrin, 2004.

Sarocchi (Jean), "Redevenir enfant", *in* Mattéi (Jean-François), (ed.), *Albert Camus et la pensée de midi*, Nice-Paris, Ovadia, 2008.

Conclusion: The Midi of Thought

ARISTOTLE, *Physics*, book II, chapter VIII, translation by P. Pellegrin, Paris, GF-Flammarion, 2000.

CAMUS (Albert), *Rivages. Revue de culture méditer ranéenne* (1938); *Le Mythe de Sisyphe, Œuvres complètes I*, Paris, Gallimard, coll. "La Pléiade", 2006.

CAMUS (Albert), "L'Exil d'Hélène" (1948), "Sur l'avenir de la tragédie" (April 29, 1955), in *Œuvres complètes III*, Paris, Gallimard, coll. "La Pléiade", 2008.

MATTÉI (Jean-François), "La tendre indifférence du monde", *in* MATTÉI (Jean-François), (ed.), *Albert Camus et la pensée de midi,* Nice-Paris, Ovadia 2008; "*L'Étranger,* entre refus et consentement", *in* MATTÉI (Jean-François), (ed.), *Albert Camus. Du refus au consentement,* Paris, PUF, 2011.

NIETZSCHE (Frédéric), "Parmi les filles du désert", *Ainsi parlait Zarathoustra,* livre IV, translation from the German by Maurice Betz, Paris, Le Livre de Poche, 1966.

SARTRE (Jean-Paul), *La Nausée*, Paris, Gallimard, 1938.

Table of contents

Best sellers Max Milo Editions

Hitler's banker, Jean-François Bouchard

Confessions of a forger, Éric Piedoie Le Tiec

The Koran and the flesh, Ludovic-Mohamed Zahed

Governing by fake news, Jacques Baud

Governing by chaos, Collectif

A political history of food, Paul Ariès

Mad in U.S.A.: The ravages of the "American model",
Michel Desmurget

Mondial soccer club geopolitics, Kévin Veyssière

Putin: Game master?, Jacques Baud

Treatise on the three impostors: Moses, Jesus, Muhammad,
The Spirit of Spinoza

TV Lobotomy, Michel Desmurget